DIY Upcycling Crafts:

25 Projects On Upcycling Old Clothes To New Stylish Outfits

Table of content

Introduction

Upcycling old clothing and making them like brand new again just makes sense for so many reasons! One of these reasons is to be able to look fashionable and stylish, without having to spend ridiculously high amounts of money on something you will only wear for one or two seasons.

Another great reason to recreate old fashions into new ones is that it is environmentally responsible. When you use what is already laying around, instead of filling up landfills with unwanted clothing, you will be doing your part to help save the planet!

Finally, you will never have to worry about showing up somewhere and finding out that someone else is wearing the exact same piece of clothing as you. Instead, you will always be able to express your unique personality in ways that will leave everyone else envious, and begging you to make something for them to wear as well.

The "DIY Upcycling Crafts: 25 Surprising Ideas on How to Take Old Clothes to Unique Modern Fashion Outfits" guide is going to teach you everything you need to know about how to redesign your clothing into today's hottest fashions. It includes patterns to create an entirely new wardrobe. You will find ideas that you can make to wear for work, play and any social occasion that shows up on your calendar.

All you need to do is follow along with each fashion pattern. As you go, you will get inspiration on how to create even more adorable tops, pants, skirts, dresses, and accessories. You may enjoy redesigning fashions so much that you choose to go into business for yourself.

Imagine, taking clothing that no one wants to wear, and making it into a fashionable item that other people will want to pay you for? Whether you are creating clothes to wear, or to sell, you are going to love what you learn in this guide.

Let's get started...

Chapter 1 – Getting Started

Welcome to the wonderful world of upcycling! You are just about ready to begin creating a brand new wardrobe for yourself that you will be able to customize to express your unique personality. Just think, not only will you look fashionable and stylish, no one else is going to look like you.

These patterns are so quick and easy, you may find that you want to make enough to share with your friends, or even start to sell them to build a part or full time income. Before you dive in though, you will want to make sure to have some necessary sewing supplies. That all starts with creating a sewing kit. You can use an actual kit or just get a shoe box to conveniently store all your items in.

Sewing Kit Essentials:

- Scissors, usually one large pair for cutting through jeans, and smaller pair to cut more intricate patterns.

- Threads of all different colors to match any fabric you are sewing.

- A collection of different sizes and styles of snaps, buttons and zippers.

- A thimble.

- A pin cushion.

- A measuring tape.

- An assortment of different sized pins and needles.

- A seam ripper to quickly rip through seams of old clothes to sew them into something new.

Speaking of having a collection of different colors of threads, you will also want an assortment of types of thread. For instance, cotton thread for sewing through denim and old t-shirts. You may also want to stock up on the following different types of threads:

- Polyester thread for sewing through stretchy types of materials.

- Silk thread for sewing through delicate fabrics.

- Metallic thread to add some pizazz.

As an upcycler, you are actually a clothing designer and it will help you to have an assortment of fabrics and accessories on hand. This way you can allow your creativity to design stunning pieces at any time. Here are some items you may want to stock up on:

- Old t-shirts, the larger the better.

- Men's button up shirts in larger sizes.

- Old jeans.

- Different types of housecoats.

- Old sweaters.

- Old pajamas.

- Décor such as patches, sequins, rhinestones, and ribbons.

- Different types of laces, even from old doilies, tablecloths or curtains.

- Fabric dye and paintbrushes.

- Chalk or fabric markers.

- Bleach Gel and sponges.

You may find other items come in handy to put the final finishing touches on your upcycled clothing. For instance, sewing silk flowers or leaves onto an old tank top in order to give it a charming statement. Because upcycling clothes is an art form, you are unlimited in the types of ideas you can come up with.

You will find a sewing machine comes in handy, but you do not have to have one. Instead, you can sew all your projects by hand if you like. Some people find this type of sewing to be a relaxing and pleasurable hobby.

Saving Money on Supplies and Old Clothes

One of the best things about upcycling old clothes is how much money you can save, while still presenting an amazing style. The first place to start, of course, is to look through your own drawers and closets. You can also ask friends and family to give you their old clothing that they know they no longer have a use for.

Garage sales and yard sales always have an abundance of old clothes that you can get for pennies on the dollar. Do not be afraid to negotiate for an even lower price. Many people will happily sell you their old clothes for a lesser amount, especially if you are going to buy more than one piece.

Second hand stores and thrift shops are another great place to find inexpensive old clothing to recreate into new masterpieces. Most of these shops have sales, and if you watch for discounts, you can save even more money.

When you have the old clothes you want to repurpose, and have the basic supplies, you are already to get started! All you need to do is pick whichever patterns you want and follow the instructions. Try them all to create a dazzling new wardrobe that you will be thrilled to just wear around the house or show off to your friends and family!

Creating an Upcycling Fashions Business

After you have worked through a few patterns, you may decide that you enjoy upcycling old clothes into new designs so much that you want to go into business for yourself. There are several ways to do this.

Selling "made to order" items is a great way to sell your fashions. This way, people can send you their measurements and you can create a piece based on what they want. Many upcyclers have found great success by creating a blog and posting examples of different fashions. Then, you can advertise that people contact you to create their orders.

Creating fashion accessories that do not depend on size, such as infinity scarves is another way to make a very nice income through doing projects that you enjoy. You can post these items on websites such as Etsy to create your own fashion shop. Advertising through social media or even your own website will make sure that sales continue to come in.

You may also want to create items to display and sell at your local craft shows, or in consignment shops.

Whether you choose to just make a few pieces for yourself, as gifts, to sell or donate, the following patterns are going to be exciting to complete. They will also teach you unlimited ways to create cutting edge fashions.

Chapter 2 – Patterns 1 through 10: Tops

Nothing is worse than showing up to work or play and finding out that someone else is wearing the same shirt that you are. Now you will never have to worry about that again. These shirt patterns will leave you looking fashionable and amazing!

Pattern 1: Polo Shirt to Boat Neck Top

Items Needed:

- Polo shirt

- Sewing kit

- Chalk or fabric marker

Instructions:

1. Cut off the collar of the polo shirt and set aside for later use.

2. Put the shirt on backward and mark where you want the boat neck neckline to fall.

3. Tear out any interfacing from the collar and save as long of a strip as possible.

4. Iron interfacing strip flat.

5. Fold interfacing strip in half with the wrong sides together and iron it flat.

6. Use folded interfacing as the ribbing for the new neckline by sewing pieces together if you need to.

7. Attach ribbing to neckline with a straight stitch.

11

8. Press neckline flat.

9. Try shirt back on and see if you want to take in the sleeves and the sides. Pin them in place.

10. Sew from the sleeves down the sides to fit.

http://www.merricksart.com/2013/02/polo-refashion-2-tutorial.html

Pattern 2: T-Shirt to Cardigan

Items Needed:

- Long sleeved t-shirt

- Sewing kit

Instructions:

1. Cut 2 inches from the middle of the front of the t-shirt.

2. Cut 2 inch strip into 1 inch strips.

3. Fold each strip around either side of the opening of the t-shirt with about 1/8 of an inch folded under and pinned.

4. Sew up strips on each side.

http://www.agirlandagluegun.com/2011/05/shirt-into-cardigan.html

Pattern 3: Knit Shirt to Embellished Tank Top

Items Needed:

- Old knit shirt

- Tank top

- Sewing kit

Instructions:

1. Cut a long strip from the bottom of the old knit shirt.

2. Fold the strip in half and cut multiple slits.

3. Roll the strip up to form into a flower shape.

4. Stitch the flower to the tank top wherever you want to, such as the upper front shoulder area.

http://thecraftingfiend.blogspot.com/2011/05/knock-off-embellished-tank.html

Pattern 4: Wedding Dress to Dressy Top

Items Needed:

- Wedding Dress

- Denim, or other fabric shirt

- Longer zipper if you need it

- Sewing Kit

http://www.threadingmyway.com/2011/12/wedding-dress-final-transformation.html

Instructions:

1. Cut the top off of the wedding dress with about 2 additional inches left on the bottom of it for hemming purposes.

2. Cut at least half of the length off the bottom of the skirt and sew in a new hem. (You can add some of the trim around the bottom of the skirt for added decor)

3. Align the top up with the skirt, so the back seams match up.

4. Sew the top and skirt together, inside out.

5. You may need to remove the zippers of each piece and add a new longer zipper.

6. Take the part of the skirt you had cut off, cut it in half and use to sew new straps onto the top.

Pattern 5: Standard T-Shirt to Updated Neckline

Items Needed:

- T-Shirt

- Sewing Kit

- Chalk or fabric marker

http://craftywimama.blogspot.com/2012/08/5-minute-upcycle-mini-project-tshirt.html

Instructions:

1. Turn the t-shirt inside out and fold in half lengthwise with the sleeves matching up.

2. Draw a faint line on the crease.

3. Sew where you marked with long stiches, from the edge of the neck down for about 5 inches.

4. Pull the thread tight to gather the material.

5. Tie the thread when you get the amount of the front of the top gathered that you want for the neckline.

Pattern 6: Man's Dress Shirt to Lady's Fashion Shirt

http://www.domesticblisssquared.com/2013/02/mens-shirt-refashion-and-mostly.html

Items Needed:

- Man's size large or extra-large button up shirt

- Sewing Kit

Instructions:

1. Take in the sides of the shirt for a more fitted waist.

2. Re-hem the bottom, adding a new, curved hemline.

3. Remove the sleeves, shorten them and re-sew them to be more fitted to your arm.

4. Wear over a t-shirt, or button up and add a belted waist.

Pattern 7: Man's Polo Shirt to Lady's Peplum Style Shirt

Items Needed:

- Man's size large or extra-large polo shirt

- Sewing Kit

Instructions:

1. Cut off the polo shirt's collar and button panel to create a rounded neckline.

2. Hem new neckline.

3. Cut straight up both side seams, including sleeves, so that all is left attached to the polo shirt is shoulder and neckline.

4. Pin shirt back together in the new tailored shape, with a slimmer waistline to a gentle flare toward the hipline.

5. Remove any excess material from the sides, but leave about an inch for the seam.

6. Sew the sides back up, inside out.

Pattern 8: Old Cardigan to Dressy Top

Items Needed:

- An old cardigan

- Sewing Kit

http://www.domesticblisssquared.com/2012/11/mens-polo-to-peplum-top-refashion.html

Instructions:

1. Cut the bottom of the cardigan off in one long strip and create a new hem.

2. Cut off the buttons and sew the front of the cardigan into a top.

3. Take the strip from the old hem and make sure both long sides are hemmed.

4. Fold one end of the strip under the neckline of the top and hem across. (Strip should be longer than the top so you have enough left over to create gathers).

5. Long stitch all the way down the hem and then pull string to gather into a ruched style. Tie off thread so the material stays gathered.

6. Sew the middle of the gathered strip to the front of the top.

Chapter 3 – Patterns 9 through 14: Pants

Whether you want to create some comfortable yoga pants for working out in, or a pair of trendy palazzo pants, the following patterns will help you do it. In fact, you may want to start a whole new wardrobe when you find out how quickly and fashionably you can repurpose your old clothes into brand new ones!

Pattern 9: Out of date Jeans to Distressed Trendy Jeans

Items Needed:

- Old jeans

- Sewing kit

- Tweezers

- Sandpaper

- Chalk or fabric marker

Instructions:

1. Try on the old jeans and use the chalk or fabric marker to outline the areas that you want to distress.

2. Sandpaper the areas on the jeans that you had marked. Then cut straight, horizontal slits over those areas, about 1/2 to 3/4 of an inch apart.

3. Pull out the vertical threads from the slits you made with the tweezers.

4. Wash and dry jeans to further distress them.

Pattern 10: Old Denim Jeans to Starry Night Fashion Jeans

Items Needed:

- Old denim jeans or shorts

- Bleach Gel

- Latex or latex alternative gloves

- Plastic cutting board

- Sewing kit

- Sponge brush

- Fabric dye

- Large star stamp

- Distressing tool, such as sandpaper, wire brush or dremel tool

Instructions:

1. Try on pants and mark the desired length. Then, cut where you had marked.

2. Put on gloves and place cutting board inside jean pant legs to create a barrier between the front and back of the pant leg.

3. Pour bleach onto a plate and dip the stamp in the bleach. Press the stamp onto front of shorts.

4. Repeat this process in a random pattern on the back of the jeans.

5. Use the sponge brush to paint bleach gel stripes on the opposite side of where you had placed the star.

6. Wash and allow shorts to dry.

7. Use fabric dye to paint according to directions, then wash and dry one more time.

http://www.upcyclingclothing.com/diy-fashion-blog

Pattern 11: T-Shirt to Yoga Pants

Items Needed:

- Large to extra-large t-shirt

- Sewing Supplies

Instructions:

1. Cut the collar off of the t-shirt by cutting straight across.

2. Cut straight up the side of the t-shirt on each side, each of these pieces will become a leg of the yoga pants.

3. Fold each leg lengthwise in half, with the right sides facing each other. Sew up the straight seam only, not the crotch or curved seam.

4. From the crotch seam, sew up to the point where the waist will start, then sew the other way to keep crotch lined up.

5. Take the sleeves of the t-shirt and cut them open at the seam, then cut them into rectangles.

6. Put each rectangle together with sides facing each other.

7. Sew the short sides of the rectangles together, to make a circle for the waist band. Add some fabric or detract some in order to fit waist.

8. Align the top of the waistband with the top of the yoga pants and fold down to sew the seams together.

9. If you need to, you can add darts or gather the material at the waistband for a better fit.

Pattern 12: Maxi skirt to Palazzo Pants

Items Needed:

- Maxi Skirt

- Sewing Kit

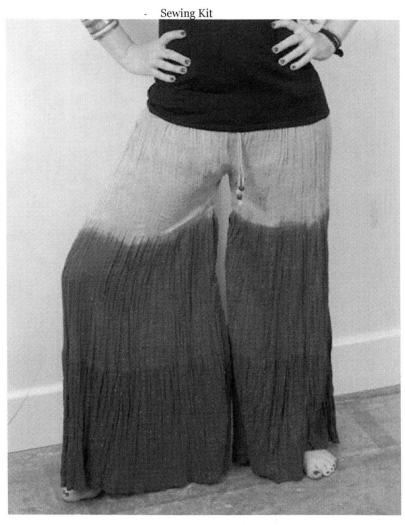

Instructions:

1. Measure your inseam with a measuring tape and leave enough extra to create the crotch seam, pin skirt to hold this place.

2. Try on the skirt carefully, with the pins in it, to make sure you measured correctly.

3. Take the skirt back off and pin down the center of the skirt from the crotch measurement down to the hemline.

4. Cut along the length of the pins.

5. Turn the skirt inside out and pin both sides of pant leg seams, then sew them up.

Pattern 13: Men's Shirt to Shorts

Items needed:

- Man's size extra-large t-shirt

- Sewing Kit

- Elastic for waistband

- A pair of shorts that fit you

- Chalk or fabric marker

Instructions:

1. Lay the t-shirt out flat.

2. Fold the shorts perfectly in half, lengthwise and line them up so the crotch of the shorts is even with the underarm sleeve of the shorts, then move them up toward the collar about 1 1/2 inches to create additional material for the seam.

3. Trace the waist of the shorts onto the shoulder or the t-shirt and add an extra inch for the waistband.

4. Cut through all the layers of the t-shirt where you had traced.

5. Pin sleeves together along the curve where the crotch will be and sew them together to make the pant legs.

6. Fold the top of the waist over and sew, leaving about 2 inches to add elastic.

7. Thread elastic through waistline and sew shut.

8. Use leftover t-shirt material to add length to the shorts if needed.

Pattern 14: Long Pants into Capris

Items Needed:

- Long pants

- Sewing kit

- Chalk or fabric marker

Instructions:

1. Try on the pants and mark about 1 inch down from where you want the length of the capris to fall.

2. Take off the pants and cut off bottom of pant legs at the chalk lines.

3. Turn pants inside out, fold about 1 inch under and hem.

Chapter 4 – Patterns 15 through 17: Skirts

For work or social events, these skirt patterns will leave you feeling as if you are ready to walk down the runway. You can easily size them for yourself, a young girl or your best friend. This way, everyone you know can soon be wearing a beautiful skirt handmade by you, with love.

Pattern 15: T-Shirt to Streamer Skirt

Items Needed:

- 2 to 3 old t-shirts
- Chalk or fabric marker
- Elastic
- Sewing kit

Instructions:

1. Flatten the t-shirt and cut off hem.
2. Cut the t-shirt into 3, 4 inch strips.
3. Measure and mark every 2 inches around the bottom of each strip.
4. Cut the strips across at the mark line, leaving about one inch at the top.
5. Repeat with the rest of the t-shirts, but only cut 2 strips each into these.
6. Cut two rectangles for the skirt's base, to fall to the desired length and width.
7. Sew up sides of the rectangles with right sides together, and then turn right-side out.

8. Run a gathering stitch through each streamer piece at the top and gather until it is the same width as the skirt's base.

9. Draw one line across the base about 1 inch from the bottom, then four more lines, 2 inches apart.

10. Attach the gathered strips from the bottom first, following the lines you drew.

11. Attach the top streamer strip with the right sides together for no stitch lines.

Pattern 16: Old Sweater to Sweater Skirt

Items needed:

- Old Sweater

- Elastic, enough to comfortably fit around your waistline

- Sewing kit

Instructions:

1. Cut the sweater straight off from under the arm pits.

2. Turn the sweater inside out and sew a seam on each side, but only if you have to take sweater in to fit better.

3. Sew a 2 inch casing around the top of skirt, leaving about 2 inches open to thread the elastic through.

4. Thread the elastic through casing to create an elastic waistline and then sew up the opening.

http://www.pearlsandscissors.com/2013/01/refashionista-sweater-into-skirt/

Pattern 17: Old jeans to Flirty Skirt

Items needed:

- Old Jeans

- Half yard of stylish fabric, cotton works best, but a polyester blend or even rayon blend also work great.

- Sewing Kit

- Chalk or fabric marker

http://ofpinksandfairytales.blogspot.com/2011/03/from-old-jeans-to-summer-skirt.html

Instructions:

1. Try on jeans and mark to just above the crotch area, leaving about 1 inch for the seam and cut the jeans at the mark.

2. Measure the bottom of the cut off area and double this value.

3. Cut two pieces of fabric to the doubled measurement from the bottom of the jeans.

4. Hem the bottoms of both pieces of fabric. Then, pin one hemmed piece to front of the jeans and one to the back.

5. Fold and pin the fabric in pleats all the way around jeans, folding the top inward to hide the raw edge.

6. Sew the fabric to the jeans, then sew both sides of fabric to each other to form skirt.

Chapter 5 – Patterns 18 through 20: Dresses

Old clothes might go out of fashion, but these dresses will quickly become classic fashions that you will want to wear time and time again. Best of all, you will not have to spend so much money on designer fashions, yet you can still look every bit as beautiful!

Pattern 18: Man's Button-Up Shirt to Peplum Dress

Items Needed:

- Man's size extra-large button up shirt

- Sewing kit

http://www.trashtocouture.com/2012/03/mens-shirt-refashion-peplum-dress.html

Instructions:

1. Use the main part of the shirt for the skirt and the bodice of the dress by sewing it up to fit.

2. Take off the sleeves, cut so they are flat and use them to create the ruffled waist.

3. Use the cuffs of the shirt to fashion the bodice's straps.

4. Use the collar of the shirt to create back sleeves to complete the peplum dress.

Pattern 19: Overly Large T-Shirts to Fringed Dress

Items Needed:

- 2 Man's size extra-large t-shirts
- Sewing kit
- Chalk or fabric marker
- Optional, tie dye, studs, or other decor

Instructions

1. Cut the collar from the first t-shirt, leaving about 3 inches on the front and back.

2. Trim corners of the first t-shirt to how you want it to sit on your shoulders.

3. Cut the second t-shirt just below the sleeves. You can use the sleeves to create fringe for the top of the first t-shirt if you want fringe on the top of the dress.

4. Pin the hem side of the second t-shirt to the hem side of the first t-shirt and then sew together.

5. Cut fringe into the bottom of the second t-shirt.

6. You can then use tie dye or other decorations to add additional style to your dress.

http://ilovetocreateblog.blogspot.com/2014/04/tie-dyed-fringe-dress-diy.html

Pattern 20: Housecoat to Dress

Items Needed:

- One housecoat

- One pair of pajama pants

- Sewing kit

- Chalk or fabric marker

Instructions:

1. Try on the housecoat and measure where you want the bodice to fall, then mark it about 1 inch lower than that to have enough fabric for the seam.

2. Cut the housecoat off at the point you marked and sew the front closed.

3. Cut the legs off of the pajama pants. Use one leg for the dress's waistline, measuring to fit your waist. You may want to double it over once or twice to give a natural backing to the waist.

4. Lay the waistline flat and start to pin house coat from the back, gently pleating as you go.

5. Sew the housecoat top to the waistline.

6. Add the second pant leg to the opening of the bottom of the housecoat to create a panel by folding about half an inch inside of the housecoat opening, pinning the pant leg to the fold and then sewing them together.

7. Cut the bottom of the pant leg so it matches the bottom of housecoat to 1 inch past desired end length.

8. Turn the 1 inch under and hem.

9. If you are making the dress fitted, you can add an invisible side or back zipper.

10. Additionally, you can remove the sleeves re-sew them for a closer fit, or leave sleeveless.

http://secondchancesbysusan.blogspot.com/2012/06/house-coat-dress.html

Chapter 6 – Patterns 21 through 25: Accessories

No outfit is complete without the perfect finishing touch. Whether you want to add a stylish infinity scarf, or some whimsical arm warmers, you will find the perfect pattern here. You might want to make enough to match every one of your outfits.

Pattern 21: Sweater to Mittens

Items Needed:

- Old sweater

- Sewing kit

- Chalk or fabric marker

Instructions:

1. Turn the sweater inside out and place flat on a firm surface.

2. Place your hands at the bottom of the sweater to where you would like the mittens to fall on your wrists. For instance, the hem of the sweater should be the line on your wrist at the length you want the mittens to cover.

3. Hold your thumb out away from your fingers to leave room for the mittens thumb space.

4. Draw a chalk outline of your hand and pin about a half inch out from that area to hold in place.

5. Cut through both sides of the sweater where the pins were placed.

6. Sew around the entire mitten area except where you will put your hands into them.

7. You can add lace around the wrists for added décor.

http://www.abeautifulmess.com/2012/01/sew-your-own-mittens.html

Pattern 22: Pajama Pants to infinity Scarf

Items Needed:

- Old pajama pants

- Sewing kit

Instructions:

1. Cut the inseam of the pajama pants and cut each leg off.

2. Lay the legs on top of each other, wrong side out.

3. Pin the bottoms of the legs together and sew them together.

4. Fold the edges of the left side and sew about 1/4 inch in, inside of itself. Pin the rest.

5. Repeat on the right side.

6. Sew where you have pinned to create an infinity scarf.

http://www.brittanymakes.com/2011/10/31/diy-flannel-infinity-scarf/

Pattern 23: Pair of Shorts to Tote Bag

Items:

Pair of shorts

Old t-shirt

Sewing kit

Instructions:

1. Cut the front of shorts away from the back.

2. Fold the back of the shorts in half to form the bag.

3. Cut 2 pieces of fabric from the t-shirt to be the same size as the bag and sew bag inside out, around all 3 sides, to create a lining.

4. Cut strips from the legs of the front pair of the shorts for the straps.

http://jembellish.blogspot.com/2011/04/bag-from-shorts-tutorial.html

Pattern 24: Socks and Lace to Arm Warmers

Items needed:

- Pair of socks

- Leftover lace

- 2 decorative buttons
- Sewing kit

Instructions:

1. Cut the toes off of each sock.

2. Gather and pin where the heel is, then hand stitch it.

3. Add decorative button to bottom of each gathered part of the arm warmers.

4. Add lace to the wrists of each arm warmer.

Pattern 25: Tank Top to iPod or MP3 Player Armband

Items Needed:

- Tank Top
- Sewing Kit
- IPod or other type of MP3 player

Instructions:

1. Measure your upper arm and add the width of the MP3 player an additional 1 1/2 inches.

2. Measure the length of the MP3 player and double that measurement.

3. Cut tank top in the width and length you measured from the bottom of the tank top.

4. Hem the top of the arm holder and fold it in half, inside, lengthwise, so it creates a tube.

5. Stitch up the length, and double it over to create a pocket for your MP3 Player.

Conclusion

By this point, you know how to recreate an entire wardrobe for yourself! You might find that you want to make 2, 3, or even 6 of each pattern to have different colors in your new, favorite outfits. As you get used to each pattern, you may also find ways to further customize it to suit your unique style to perfection!

Remember these steps for the best results:

- Create a sewing kit.

- Add additional décor items to your sewing kit collection.

- Stay on the lookout for bargains to save money, while you create the hottest new styles.

- Make extra for family, friends and to sell.

Best wishes for upcycling a beautiful and fashionable new you!